This book is dedicated to all Parents especially to those who Wish to be Families on Christmas & who believe in the spirit of the Holidays, & to their families, & friends.

This book is written for children. This story will help us to remember that Holidays & Christmas are a time for family & friends and being thankful for all that we have.

Education is the key to understanding. I believe that the publication of this book will promote a reminder of the importance of Family celebrations and goodwill towards men during the Holidays.

I would like to Thank Everyone for their Inspiration, support and opportunities they have provided.

Written & Illustrated by:
Micheline Abounassar
(artist micha)
©Copyright 2017 & 2022
All rights reserved.

no portion of this book may be reproduced, by any process or technique, without the express written consent of Micheline Abounassar

It was a night before Christmas, when all around the World, the sky was night & everyone was waiting for Santa to arrive the next day.

All the Children around the World were sleeping in their beds, waiting for Christmas day.

And as always, in the North Pole, Santa & Mrs. Clause and all of Santa's Elves were busy preparing the Children's Gifts.

For Santa had very Special requests & wanted to make sure he delivered all the presents to everyone that asked him for a Special Gift.

But one very different request
was sitting on Santa's desk.

It was a letter from a young boy named
Charlie Green that seemed to capture
Santa's heart and attention

And so, the letter read: "Dear Santa... I would like to ask you for one Wish this Christmas! I wish that my mother will be well so that she can come home for Christmas!"

After preparing all the presents for the Children around the World, Santa now focused on Charlie's Wish.

With a tear in his eye, Santa was touched that Charlie did not want any presents, but rather he wanted his mom to be well & with him at Christmas.

Santa called his friends where Charlie's mom had been at a hospital near Charlie's home.

From monetary gifts that Santa had received to help, Santa offered to pay for Charlie's mom's medications, so that she can recover & come home for Christmas.

The very next day, Santa delivered all the presents to all the Children around the World.

But before going back to the North Pole, Santa made one last stop: at Charlie's house of course.

Not only did Santa want to Wish Charlie and his mom and Family a very Merry Christmas, but he also brought another special gift for Charlie & his mom.

Santa arrived at Charlie's home, with bells in his hand, and Rudy in the snow.

Santa hugged Charlie and said, "Charlie, you are a very Special boy indeed."

"For all that you asked for was for your mother to be well this Christmas so you can be together. I am very proud of you Charlie, you have a special kind heart."

Santa continued, "And because of this, I have brought you additional presents."

Charlie looked at Santa with his big brown eyes and said, "But Santa, what could possibly be more than having my mom here with me.."

Santa replied, "Well, Charlie, you are right, there is no greater gift than having your mom & family around for Christmas!"

CHRISTMAS
MOM
CHARLIE

"And so, I am here to tell you that from now on, you can expect to Celebrate many more Christmases with your mom"

21

"For we have found the way to help your mom receive her medications at home so you will not have to worry ever again"

22

MAGIC MIRACLE

Excited and jumping in Joy, Charlie could not believe the miracle he had heard from Santa. It was truly Magical indeed. There is always someone who will help you in any situation.

And so, with "Faith, Hope, & Love" Charlie now was even more excited about Christmas than ever before.

Santa said, "Charlie, I want to Thank you for reminding everyone of the meaning of Christmas!"

"And there is one more present that i want to give you," said Santa to Charlie.

"This is a savings account in your name that will help you to also go to College when you are old enough, so that you can find a job to also help your mom.

"And one last thing: because you thought about your mom before yourself, i have brought to you & your mom many presents & toys to enjoy this Christmas!"

Again with joyful tears in his eyes, Charlie said, "Thank you very much Santa for giving us the true meaning of Christmas, that is "to love one another and cherish our time in faith & family."

And so now Everyone around the World was happy, and Celebrating Christmas with their families. Santa was now filled with Joy as he went back to the North Pole.

The End

ABOUT THE AUTHOR: TALENTED HAND & GIVING HEART
Micheline Abounassar (artist micha)

Entrepreneur/Founder/CEO/Artist/Writer/Philanthropist/etc
Michasgallery.com

Among some of the dignitaries and charitable organizations that have received her paintings include the Pope in the Vatican, Jay Leno & Harley Davidson Love Ride Foundation, Mda, SNL, Simon Cowell & America's Got Talent Productions, Howie Mandel, Philanthropists Billionaires Carlos Slim Helu & Gilbert Chagoury: St. Jude Children's Hospital Ambassador. TCL Chinese Theatres Owner & Producer Elie Smaha; the Special Olympics, Hospitals, Cathedrals & St. Patrick's Cathedral in New York, Museums, City of Hope, Producers, Beverly Hills, CA, Writers, Actor Bradley Whitford, Mother Angelica at EWTN, H.E. Cardinal Leonardo Sandri, Doctors, Sheriffs, and many other high profile Celebrities & non-profit organizations. Televised to millions of viewers worldwide on TV, in magazines, newspapers, etc: see also her wall of awards & accolades & Latimes stories at michasgallery.com ...

Born around midnight in summer of 1980, Micheline Abounassar is a renowned fine artist and writer to the stars, & spends most of her years working her **Artistic Magic** in her tiny Glendale California studio gallery room for over 20 years. She has won several first place awards for her art & writing since the age of 5 till date. Bringing awareness with her paintings & books that are diverse with all subjects: people, pets, landscapes, seascapes, etc., as well as working with many renowned diverse charitable organizations.

She is a descendant of the Durighello family, who enriched the Louvre museum in France. Her entrepreneurial spirit is reflected in her charitable donations that come from sales of her work. The Mda Muscular Dystrophy Association also auctioned one of her art paintings print for a huge hit of $17,000 (100% of proceeds went to charity).

Ingram Content Group UK Ltd.
Milton Keynes UK
UKHW020744080623
423003UK00002B/6